T0303666

more praise for
PHOENIX SONG

"Lose yourself in this delightfully queer volume, oozing with subversion, kaleidoscopic truth, and shimmering unicorn energy. Here around the sparkling, flickering rainbow fire LD Green has created, you will find yourself staring into the healing flames, and you'll know that you're not alone. Whether exploring radical mental health, the complex spectrum of trans identity, the lingering effects of trauma, or the liberation of bi experience, Green's prose and poetry made me feel seen and honored in a way I have not experienced for a long time in the pages of a book. *Phoenix Song* is not just a chapbook; it is a soothing balm in words, centering and elevating the lived experiences of those who have all too often found themselves at the margins."

L. Harris
writer, facilitator,
and mental health advocate

"In *Phoenix Song*, LD Green constructs an abiding sense of personal identity, excavating meaning from the ashes of intimate traumas, losses and momentary feelings of inner disintegration and confronting the painful, more often than not unaddressed complexities of mental health and the psychiatric miscategorization of inherent states of being. A beautifully profound and rewarding read."

Ellery Washington

professor of writing at the Pratt Institute,
author of *Buffalo*

"LD Green's *Phoenix Song* travels across identity to ambitiously explore sexuality, gender, mental health and healing. However, that ambition never eclipses the heart of this hybrid collection: its tenderness, its humor, its crystalline need to commune and marvel in our complex human experience. You can feel the love in these pages."

Miah Jeffra

St. Lawrence Book Award
and Prairie Schooner Book Prize finalist for
The Violence Almanac

"A beautiful, poignant, and resilient collection of poetry and prose exploring the intersections of gender, sexuality, mental health, and being embodied."

Julia Serano

author of *Whipping Girl: A Transsexual Woman on Sexism and the Scapegoating of Femininity* and *Excluded: Making Feminist and Queer Movements More Inclusive*

"LD Green whispers healing tears into their *Phoenix Song*. With the alchemy of a herd of unicorns, they transform other people's narratives of their childhood trauma and psychiatric dis-ease into an anthem of survivorship, a reclamation of dangerous gifts, and a fantastical recockinging with identity. Unapologetic, non-binary, and quippy, Green takes the reader on a journey of melodic freedom and revelations that scorch untruths about gender, sexuality, mental health, and love. This rebirth is tender, bold, funny and heart touching. A true gift from a writer who shares, 'my nature is to burn.'"

Kelechi Ubozoh

Co-Editor of *We've Been Too Patient*

NOMADIC PRESS

OAKLAND

111 FAIRMONT AVENUE
OAKLAND, CA 94611

BROOKLYN

475 KENT AVENUE #302
BROOKLYN, NY 11249

WWW.NOMADICPRESS.ORG

MASTHEAD

FOUNDING PUBLISHER
J. K. FOWLER

ASSOCIATE EDITOR
MICHAELA MULLIN

EDITOR
MIAH JEFFFRA

DESIGN
JEVOHN TYLER NEWSOME

MISSION STATEMENT

Through publications, events, and active community participation, Nomadic Press collectively weaves together platforms for intentionally marginalized voices to take their rightful place within the world of the written and spoken word. Through our limited means, we are simply attempting to help right the centuries' old violence and silencing that should never have occurred in the first place and build alliances and community partnerships with others who share a collective vision for a future far better than today.

INVITATIONS

Nomadic Press wholeheartedly accepts invitations to read your work during our open reading period every year. To learn more or to extend an invitation, please visit: www.nomadicpress.org/invitations

DISTRIBUTION

Orders by teachers, libraries, trade bookstores, or wholesalers:

Nomadic Press Distribution
orders@nomadicpress.org
(510) 500-5162
nomadicpress.org/store

Small Press Distribution
spd@spdbooks.org
(510) 524-1668 / (800) 869-7553

Phoenix Song
© 2022 by LD Green

This book was made possible by a loving community of chosen family and friends, old and new.

For author questions or to book a reading at your bookstore, university/school, or alternative establishment, please send an email to info@nomadicpress.org.

Cover art: Arthur Johnstone

Published by Nomadic Press, 111 Fairmount Avenue, Oakland, California 94611

First printing, 2022

Library of Congress Cataloging-in-Publication Data

Title: *Phoenix Song*
p. cm.
Summary: *Phoenix Song* has many recurring themes—non-binary gender, queer and bi+ sexuality, and childhood and psychiatric trauma. As the traumas resonate within the speaker, we understand them as the root of mental health struggles—rather than clinical, problematic psychiatric "diagnosis." As the speaker moves from lyrical embodiment of deep feeling to the clarity of prose, they are set free and return, renewed by flame, to the joys of pleasure and their song. It's true we are all the heroes of our own stories, but we are also sometimes part of something bigger—a bright, sparkling, magic, urgent wave of not-so-delicate beasts, cresting through the water, a surge, a collective: "me too." This collection offers an incantation, a wisdom synthesized by both mind and body.

[1. POETRY / Subjects & Themes / Mental Health. 2. POETRY / Subjects & Themes / Healing. 3. POETRY / LGBTQIA+. 4. POETRY / Non Binary. 5. POETRY / American / General.] I. III. Title.

LIBRARY OF CONGRESS CONTROL NUMBER: 2021949443

ISBN: 978-1-955239-20-2

PHOENIX SONG

LD GREEN

PHOENIX SONG

LD GREEN

NOMADIC PRESS

CONTENTS

introduction

reading guide

INTRODUCTION

As a small child, I watched a lot of epic fantasy movies. Well, two, mainly: *The Last Unicorn* and *The Neverending* Story. I used to joke that I watched and rewatched these two so much that their themes and symbols were imprinted into my psyche. Probably true.

Then round about college time, when I should have been studying, I got high with friends and watched these movies again. The big takeaway from one friend was that in *The Neverending* Story, The Nothing represented capitalism. And sure, I've definitely railed against the 1% with the best of them.

But the symbolism of *The Last Unicorn* has probably been the defining narrative of my life, culminating in this book's publication (my own neverending story...)

I want to credit my excellent friend Meredith Summs for correctly identifying the villain of that movie as the Red Bull...of cisheteropatriarchy patriarchy. He wants the unicorns (marginalized genders) trapped forever for his amusement and under his control in the ocean near his tower. The last one, she is not last, or lost, at all. She defeats the Red Bull, frees the other unicorns.

It's true we are all the heroes of our own stories, but when I recall the enchantment and lasting impression of my own childlike wonder, it is this image: the bright, sparkling, magic, urgent, and not-so-delicate

beasts, cresting through the water, a surge, a collective—a wave.

Tarana Burke had the spark, and her song consisted consisted of two words: me too.

We are a wave. I am in this wave. I am powerful only because I am not alone in the unleashing of truth—a potent magic.

This book shares some traumas—childhood and psychiatric. Sometimes they are coded lyrically, sometimes they are more plain spoken in prose as part of a framework for understanding the needs for mental health care reform. (CW: I am not graphic with regards to childhood trauma, though I do embody its experience through metaphor, and I do delineate some psychiatric traumas.)

But if this wave of unicorns is the unifying image of the book, you best trust that it's also pretty damn gay.

And what of the phoenix? This book has work in it that's been with me over a decade, and work that's as fresh as a skinned knee. The phoenix rose and fell through cycles of ash and fire and flight several times in the gestation of this book, and they are finally ready to settle in for the long haul, and sing.

For Ramon(a), with love and gratitude

We look before and after,
And pine for what is not;
Our sincerest laughter
With some pain is fraught;
Our sweetest songs are those that tell
Of saddest thought.
Percy Shelley

I cannot name this
I cannot explain this
And I really don't want to
Just call me shameless
Ani DiFranco

In order to rise from its own ashes, a Phoenix first must burn.
Octavia Butler

APPLES AND ORANGES

When I was 16, I went on a mental trip.
I was convinced that if I ate oranges, everyone would know I liked
girls. But if I chose an apple instead, I would land only in boys' beds.
But this wasn't acid—this was

      psychosis.

          So I wrote this—

for every queer who spent their teenage years in fear,

and especially for the ones like me,
raised on the buckle of the Bible belt,
who felt their yearning splinter
like a broken mirror:
I want both!

Apples and oranges...
But by now it seems painfully obvious to me what I should have done:

Come out, join the fun!

So I moved to San Francisco.
And the minute I landed north of the Mason-Dixon line,
I went south...of a girl's panty line.

But somewhere between my thighs—
Still—is that Oklahoma teen whispering—

*I'm sorry! I didn't mean to! I want—The drama club king, drunk on
Applejack. I want only his fierce funny laughter and none of that...soft
flute player, trilling her tongue across the passion of her breath—and oh
if that were only my neck...but I certainly can't hold both of you inside my
hopechest—No.*

I must choose...between apples and oranges.

I can't take a girl for a whirl
and make a boy my toy
because that would destroy...

      the prom picture.

And I know it sounds trite,

a broken record from 1995,
but I have had eleven years of movement
away from that red dirt, and I'm telling you:

the dirty blood dust left a film on my skin. A tornado took hold of
my mind, and said: *you'll never be the same again.* Competing desires
pulled me in bipolar directions, and the weathervane spun like a
journey, like a lesson. And all I can say now to these memories, these
flashes...is to

kiss. their. wind.

and watch them fall

into dust, into ashes.

Because an Oklahoma storm can tear the roof off your house.
And an Oklahoma town can rip you in two.

But the air is so much sweeter after that storm is through.
And it's true, my breakdown was not a hate crime.
It wasn't my body left crucified in a Wyoming field.

But in a town where crosses are taller than water towers,
without the lord as my shepherd,
I could not walk out of the valley of doubt
 into a calmer plain of existence
without first falling headlong into a nightmare madness
that stretched my soul across a fence.

And it took Haldol, it took Zoloft...

No.

It took poetry. It took punk rock.
It took Sylvia Plath, Kathleen Hanna,
and a hot Jewish dyke from Connecticut.
It took years before I could stand on this stage and
act. out. now. and call. out. proud.

Because when I tasted the apple, I didn't taste sin...
And when I swallowed an orange slice,
my hunger was satisfied.

So I know now whatever state I'm in, it doesn't matter if it's
South, North, West, or East
When I see fruit
I see a feast.

EVENT HORIZONS

1.

A young man tells me I don't belong—I'm going to the women's restroom, he yells "Miss!" Then asking "Man?" No sincerity in this, cis man, but you announce my scissored self, and you run recklessly with it. I retreat, head down into a text message that does not send until later, I escape into a secluded stall, release my refuse, and return to sharp laughter. Into the black hole I go. It's a tight squeeze. I'd rather be wearing a compression vest.

2.

A colleague asks if I want to help with Women's History Month. We whisk away in Dr. Who's (Gender) Police Call Box and visit the cis body I once was (Was I ever cis?...but she doesn't know we tripped—outing is slow going). What has Women's History done for me? What have I done for women? I am not a woman. I'm the Doctor. My brain pulses between two hearts. She wants me to join her in reprising *The Vagina Monologues* on campus again, like we did two years ago... remember when? Remember when I suspended my misgivings with suspenders? Remember when I uttered "cunt" but it exploded like a bizarre supernova? I tell her I would. I tell her I would. I told her I would. I would but no. I would but can we write a preface about its limitations? I would but know—it doesn't fit me anymore. If it ever did. I don't say this though. I should. Here space and time narrows to a pinpoint, my mass goes into collapse.

3.

The definition of woman is slippery. The definition of woman is hard. "Anyone who identifies and presents as a woman" qualifies for this event. Neither, no. *Yes, both, if it means I get to speak!* Oh, hello, you, young sweet companion, you've ridden with me a long time now. You've always been here, head against both my hearts, searching for a rhythm you can dance to. This is my body, love. This is my chest and head and lanky attachments. And this is your body, too. I know you aim to please. I know you want praise. I think it's time you let me hold you and soothe you, little girl inside this boy-man chest. Wait for it. We have so many more event horizons ahead.

4.

You will make it through them intact. You can act. You will not collapse, you will compress, yes, wear that vest, shape shift, same ship in a box, same looping music, same purple swirls surround as you descend, narrow go go go, and then emerge, fresh, new Doctor body, another way of moving, a new universe on the other side of this black hole, this portal let's go—

5.

Only the hesitation causes the collapse.

LADY MACBETH TO OCTOMOM

My womb was drier than a bone.
As fertile as the Dead Sea.
This was a blessing, you fool.
At least we had that in common once.
Then you installed a sprinkler system in your tubes
that would put Dubai to shame.
It's more than a waste.
Fourteen children curl around you—
fat snakes, sucking food and fuel
from a world sick with the lack of ambition.

I had guts.
What do you have?
Tumors. Living, shitting cancers.
And no, I don't hate all children.
They can be useful.
But your infants are born of a science
That gives feast
Where there should be famine.
Some women are not meant to be mothers—
These women must grasp other things.
Are you sick with estrogen?

I was the bit inside my husband's mouth,
the spur in his flank
the reigns, and yes the whip.
And oh, I rode him well.
Rode him right off his rocker...
And mine too.

I used a stronger force than offspring
To control my husband.
But do not mistake my courage
for manhood.
I carved myself into a queen chess piece:
glass and ivory chiseled hips
my breasts give me life
no burden

I used my body well:
Kill him, Macbeth, and you can touch me
Kill her, Macbeth, and you can enter me
Kill, Macbeth, and you will have me

But don't you see? I was not a woman possessed!

I had him. He was *mine*.
And through him, on him, I could ride,
charge through the gates
of any castle and eat:
meats, fruits, thick cakes, and then,
my shape would finally soften
the edges blur round
My belly full.

I would be woman, then.
Perhaps I could have held my blood even
Perhaps like you I could have found some witch
to cast a spell
make me eight times the woman you are
and no more Lady.
no more bony hips and diamond tits,
I'd have breasts full with giving
...and children.
What it must be like to hold something gently,
to support its fragile neck.
I can't imagine wanting this—
But then, I couldn't keep my own life.

But were I you:
Were I born yesterday,
I would cherish my empty womb
I would not force blood
from everyone else
to make up for my lack
I would not wash my hands
all day and curse the spot of red
I would turn the fight on me instead.
I would hold my own daggers
See them before me:
The choice I would now have
I would grab the metal
by the blade
I would cut myself on my ambition,

flipping the dagger around like a deft jester,
now holding it right,
holding it high
I would carve off my useless breasts
and make myself a man
because in this time,
in your world, I can.

I would scar my own flesh
Before I kissed another death
Because that's the shape of things I wanted:
Not to sit beside his throne,

But to *be* King Macbeth.

So once I slip inside the suit, so svelte and neat,
I'd sit down with you,
and your eight crying heads,
I'd hold them,
burp them,
to give you a little relief.

But I must ask you:
Why poison yourself with joy?
I know of this need to collect bodies—
to hold them as you do
or to bury them as I did.
Neither of us can escape:
our body counts will not make up
for the power we lack.

BODY TO MACHINE

When I bought my car from an attractive man off craigslist, I was pretty sure I was getting a good deal. Especially since he noted, multiple times, that:

"I've never had a problem with this car starting. It always starts. Yes. Very reliable. Did I mention it always starts? Never dies, nope. Not this car."

A couple times the car did have trouble starting, but only after I'd done something stupid like left the lights on for several hours. Many times I have had to depend on the jumper cables and kindness of strangers.

A few years ago, while driving to a bar with a touring DJ, my car completely collapsed. A sudden heart attack, no life left whatsoever: no dashboard lights, no clock, no hazards, nothing. Now, this was just too much. I had done nothing wrong, I had respected and honored my car's exacting demands. This couldn't be retaliation for anything. He had just up and left me, for no good reason. Luckily my passenger was clever enough to guide a wire from the battery back to its proper place, and without much fanfare or drama, we were back on the road again. We flirted and kissed, and I took her home. She was as serviceable as a spark plug. Though we didn't get fully under the hood because, well, I have to hesitate sometimes. I know my ignition can be a little sticky, after the grease left there when I was a child. So sometimes, I barely turn the key.

Other times, I know I'm ready to rev the engine.

A few weeks later, I drove a boy to the top of Grizzly Peak, otherwise known as Inspiration Point. It's a classic make-out destination, the Berkeley hills overlooking the lights of the bridges and Bay Area cities. I met him at concert with friends. We shared snide remarks and I liked the way he laughed with his whole body. He touched my waist, held my hips. We did the liquor dance. This was heavy pheromone activity. We moved too closely together, lips brushing past necks, for this to be mere number exchange time. I assumed we were due for at least a little make-out session. More, if I could discern he wasn't worth dating, but at least worth one good night. One small hitch: rewind to standing outside the house: Did he say he knew that girl through...his *girlfriend's* sister? Well...he says he loves Ani DiFranco. I must have misheard him.

So we made it to Inspiration Point. We hovered over my iPod, bonding over Indigo Girls music. He touched my stomach, then my leg. I gave him that look that says, *Whenever you're ready...*

Finally, he sighed and said, "Maybe you're wondering why I seem so pained."

"Are you seeing someone?"

"Yes. But—in my mind, there's a line between what we've been doing and kissing you, and if I kissed you it would be cheating."

Now, at some level, I guess I felt responsible. I *had* heard him when he uttered that typically prohibitive word, "girlfriend" and had let myself do the liquor dance anyways. That doesn't mean he wasn't a shitty little tease, but I couldn't really pin him to the wall. He had that moment of disclosure on his side. I could have lied and said I had never heard that word and insisted on his treachery and deception. But high drama isn't my style with flings. I save that for the long haul, for those who endure life's difficulty with me. It's their reward for sticking it out. So after a few moments of frustrated sighs and half-hearted attempts to break him (*well, she's across the country and he says they're having trouble and dammit we've come this far!*), I realized I didn't really want to be that girl, and furthermore, I didn't have time for this wishy-washy shit. I put the key in the ignition.

The dashboard lights came on. The engine groaned but wouldn't turn over. Just a little bellyache moan, but no juice. The car was dead on the top of Grizzly Peak, and here I was with a man too spineless to carry through an affair and too heartless to resist me completely. A spineless, heartless, lesbian-folk loving, sensitive new-age guy who I still wanted to bang all the more because I knew it was *bad*. Nice guys can be nasty little creatures. They're just so terribly familiar.

He leaned into me and said, "Well I guess we're going to spend the night together after all."

Now I wanted to get the hell out. We tried pushing the car and popping the clutch. We debated the best exit strategy, but as it was four in the morning, we figured it would be safer to wait until sunrise. I was not thrilled at the idea of flagging down a car in the middle of the night or paying fifty dollars for a tow truck. The sun would rise in two hours, so it seemed the best option to wait until the morning go-getters would replace the late-night party people. In the meantime, he suggested we huddle together in the backseat. For warmth. *Right.*

But after all, it was cold...

Naturally, I hadn't wanted him half as much until I found out he was off limits, just outside of my reach. He was tied to the bedposts of commitment and I was handcuffed by abstract solidarity with a woman I'd never met. To him, I was an olive. He stole me from the bar, but I was not the food that gave him strength. He had his girlfriend for that. To me, he was a well-deserved shift drink after a long night of hard flirting. He touched my belly again, this time bare. He was surprised to find muscles under my beauty marks.

I drew up to slide a tongue across his neck. Pushing me flat on my back, he said, "I like torturing you." The fury in my hand collapsed, shaky and loose. He tied the ropes tighter with a look that said: *Let me wake up every nerve, every shred of feeling, until you pulse and ache and dream about me for days.* Let me consume you. We touched. We talked. Mostly, we talked about not touching. So "nothing" happened. But there was a tender mercy in this torture.

We finally left the following morning by getting some advice from passing bicyclists on how to pop the clutch.

He got out, leaned hard against the trunk. He pushed me and my reluctant car slowly down a hill and I forced the thing to start from a higher gear. It did the trick.

I dropped him off and he thanked me for the music, called me later to assuage his guilt.

I travel around in a body that has been molested. I don't hate my body, but the experience has, amongst other things, made it sometimes more difficult to get turned on. I travel around in a car that never seems to start when I want it to. The only way I've found to fix the problem is by chance, the right spark, the right strategy for the moment. Maybe a wire needs subtle movement, guidance by an artist's hand. But sometimes, you need to get out of the car and push, body to machine, and whip it into submission.

CODA

What I should tell you about him is that he kept texting. What I should tell you about me is that I texted back. What I should tell you about this story, is that it's true, down to our Halloween costumes of the last night I saw him.

While he was texting me and I wasn't responding, I bought a book called *Against Love: A Polemic*—a Marxist diatribe against monogamy—and obsessed over him for a couple weeks. Eventually, I relented to his texts. We got some pizza, nothing happened. I mean, nothing happened that night at Grizzly Peak, too right? But even less nothing. He might have lifted me up in the air. He might have flattered me. I might have liked it.

He died a year later in a motorcycle accident, the only person I've known to die from an automobile crash. A mutual friend called me after it happened.

"I know you have mixed feelings about him, but I thought you should know...he was traveling in Sri Lanka and he was riding his motorcycle. It was an isolated road. He made a turn too fast. He...he didn't make it."

I paused on the other end, pulling onto the freeway, passing the BART station. I heard the pain in her voice. They'd been roommates. I hadn't thought about him in some time, though. "I'm so sorry...are you okay?"

"Yes, it's sad, but I have people to talk about it with. I'm just telling you because there's going to be a West coast memorial. His funeral's back east. I thought you might want to go. It will be at our old house. Next Tuesday. You can bring a candle, we're going to share stories...just remember him."

"Well thank you, but I don't think that would be the place for me."

"Well, think about it."

"I will."

I didn't go. I probably should have.

The last time I saw him was at a bar in the Mission on Halloween.

He had his face and naked torso painted like a brick wall. He smiled and moved in to hug me, but then retreated. "I'll probably stain your suit. Who are you?"

I looked down, as if I'd forgotten. "Oscar Wilde," I said, twirling my cane and patting my ascot.

"Clever," he said. He gestured to the bar, and we sat down, ordered some beers.

"I turned our night into a story," I said, sipping my drink.

"Really?! Do you make me seem like an asshole?"

I softened. I told him to make an overture to friendship, not to confront him or make him feel guilty. "You're fine. It takes two to tango." I smiled.

He smiled back, and we enjoyed some pleasant conversation. I only noticed later that the paint of his hand had left a mark on my collar. *Godspeed, fellow wanderer.*

SOMETIMES I SLIP

They say when you see a wild beast, the last thing
You should ever do is make yourself small.
Don't tremble.
Raise your arms like you're calling down lightning,
Scream.
Let your voice echo through the canyon.

Forty five years ago, a man died here, trying to kill a grassfire.
He was the solitary doctor in a sanitarium.
These fields used to cradle a crazy house.
When shipped to Wildcat Canyon,
You would be safely quarantined.
Miles from the disgrace of a loving family.
This was not vacation. This was a colony.
And the doctor ran it, for forty three years.
Until fire consumed him in his effort to beat it back.

I have vacationed in spots like this before.
Four times in my life, I have been too patient
with the good intentions of this secular priesthood.
I held my mouth open to commune with the corporate body
While my blood was measured to determine
The diagnosis of my curse.

But today I am only a spectator to these specters,
I do not believe the patterns in the grass to hold any more truth
Than a passing laugh, and mine is not maniacal.
But every day I live with the fear that the mirror will see
That the predator is me.

I can only hold myself back from the edge
of the canyon so long
until it's the effort itself, the awkward shaking,
the denial of my desire to jump
feet first into the unknown—
That makes me small.
Makes me tremble.
Makes me look like prey.

So today I choose to raise my hands high,
like I can call down rain.
Maybe some kind of lightning caused that grassfire,
but only water and time can make things right.

Lightning does strike in the same place twice,
But each time I was institutionalized
In a synthetic expansion of adolescent nights,

I howled at the sun and gathered fruit under the moon,
Grew fangs as a mouse and the wolf in me trembled.
Hunting my own flesh and gathering his
This distortion of civilization has rendered wrong
Every action along the both poles of my reason
Into dueling serpents of logic and feeling
I must be spreading some kind of treasonous disease,
Something to quarantine.
So what will you call me?
When the sky opens next time,
When everything I say becomes
Indecipherable rhyme.
Those adolescent nights did not
Shudder off into a dawn the color of Depakote.
I walk carefully around my edges to avoid this, but
Sometimes
I slip. I'm only
                    human.

POMEGRANATE

1. Just Three Seeds

Rabbit with human teeth. "Creepy," I said. "Don't worry, I agree," he said. But you're still holding the puppet—relentless—still saying— you're awesome, I miss you and where were you when my signal went out at midnight? Could you not hold me, at least, in your teeth? "You know, radio frequencies," he said. "Conspiracy theories," we fondled. We thought of fucking. But because of safety we decided to be dangerous. Tasted illicit the fruit like wonderbread but moldy but it's ok this time it's just like home. I miss you and where were you that night? When I held a pen against my heart darkly. When you wore black, when I wanted to be Batman's daughter. I just wanted a taste this time, just three seeds. Because sometimes, in California, I miss the winter.

2. Emerge for Now

Often it is honeysuckle; my dream softens my forehead. Often I have a rare moment of opening, suck the nectar, balm, muggy day. When I shyly glimpse and curl a mouth towards topsoil. These blossoms, so disposable, so indispensable. Countless buds, overgrown and tempting, say—"sicken yourself here, on autumn, on reap." The stems poke out, embarrassed and bare as yellow petals are vacuumed up with childish lips. Learn to sample. Learn summer. Learn seasonless cycles of rain, dry, growth. Learn humid: stand in it, sleeveless, no shy armpit. Just sweat, nectar, momentary sustenance.

Abundance now, of everything that teases.

3. Return and Face the Dead

The strange love fist that only rises in anger. With you. Rises with my anger, your heart, a buoy, a tide, a starfish. Never bruising—right? This strange love fist erupts for the sake of connection, wants to make alien babies out of stomach lining and paperweights. I cannot hold you down (there) any longer. Explode, somewhere, please—don't ask me to make you beautiful. That is the work. That is breakfast and noontime as respite. That is physical, gardens of muscular petals, that is, where did I put my manifesto? Yes, there, it's due next Tuesday. You are only ugly. You hollow scream, you bitter, accidental grace— only what I need to say—you—must be—No, I must make you, find you, shush you, pillowfight and cottonwrap you, I must absorb you. (Abolish you! Extract, extract, extract.) I must you. Must. You. Scrape. I. Together. Sing.

FINDING THE SIGNAL

STATIC

Tasted illicit the fruit like wonderbread but moldy but it's ok this time it's just like home.
Explode, somewhere, please—don't ask me to make you beautiful.

STATIC

If people wanted you to write warmly about them,
they should have behaved better.

STATIC

The easiest way to play the game of Hearts
Is to lose every heart you gain.
But if you're feeling reckless and a little bit shrewd,
You turn the game on its head,
Hold every heart instead...
This is called shooting the moon.
This is a game my Grandma taught me to play,
Her tiny frame bearing down on the competition
Like a bent safety pin, ready to burst

You see, both Grandma Dorothy and the Queen of Spades
blessed and cursed you in the same breath,
Kissed with contradiction:
The queen's presence means 13 points
in a game where less is more.

Her wit, wisdom, and power
Held inside the Mormon Church like a frozen flower
I told her I was abused.
She believed the story
But not my truth, not that it was—

I forgot I—

STATIC STATIC STATIC STATIC STATIC

I FORGOT I REMEMBERED

Battle not with monsters, lest ye become a monster. And if you gaze into the abyss, the abyss gazes also into you.
Friedrich Nietzsche

He always held a camera.

Focus.

That one time,
He handed me the lens backwards.

I have looked at that event
this way—
For 31 years.

Time lapse.

"Blurry" doesn't begin.

I have a burning wound.
Red.

Indistinct through the frame.
I can't see it, but the heat of it cools
over time, with care and airing.

For years, I tried to imagine how I was hurt.
(Did he do it? Best guess.)
And when? Did I forget?
I assumed so.

Exposure compensation.

My conscious memory seemed to lack an event.
(Except...that one time...)
I trusted my body and believed myself,
Believed the memory was buried.

I wrote a novel over eleven years
(not knowing I was trying)
to find the answer
Hiding in code, in plain sight.

Long exposure.

My hero molested at exactly—

Eleven Eleven
(11:11)

I titled the book this, too—
These numbers became my obsession

Why?
I couldn't say until a few weeks ago.
Suddenly:

Oh, that's right. I've always known this.
Always remembered what I swore I forgot.
Just turn the lens around, LD.

Turn the lens.

I was eleven.
(eleven, eleven...)

He was...not.

Four screams in my life, four interruptions
Cut through space-time
The most elaborate ruses
I concocted about the eyes and hands of God and government?

I believed them—I knew
I was watched, mishandled.
They locked me up with more mirror games
And panopticon terrors.

                                              Depth of field.

But it began with him—
The million cuts of his gaze
The one dagger,

That one time.

You had no right to look at me
Or touch me
The way you did.

                                              Shutter release.

I do not think him a monster.
But I have battled his shadows,
All these long years.

I let that go now.

At last, I direct myself—   Cast my gaze away from the abyss.

PHOENIX SONG, VERSE ONE: THE STIRRING BIRD

You own everything that happened to you. Tell your stories. If people wanted you to write warmly about them, they should have behaved better. **Anne Lamott**

(for Kelechi Ubozoh)

The teacher handed me an egg—
Light blue, delicate shell, the stirring bird
Curled warm in my palm, I could feel them.

The teacher said:

...they should have behaved better.

I put the egg in my mouth.
I couldn't speak.

So I found a box
Full of hay and sneezing
(I told myself a fragile thing needed straw)
I put the box in my attic of dust and dark

Then, I met you
We laughed our birdsong
And you knew what I had in store.
I gave you the box
For safekeeping

I told you what the teacher said:
They should have behaved better

We laughed our way out of the attic
To a meadow, to the sun.

We met again one day, years later
You whispered the words she gave me,
Palm up, holding the egg
The bird stirred again.

Peck, peck,
Crack, crack,
A phoenix sang
Eager to live their fire life
Unafraid of shadows or shame
Knowing their light matters more.

PHOENIX SONG, VERSE TWO: FROZEN MENAGERIE

1. Unicorn

Lying in the hospital bed on Thorazine, she remembers her reflection in a silver puddle. She recalls the shape of her face. Her crown, her horn. Her lavender mane and tail, her bright white moon coat. Now, she is naked, a slender ape. So fragile. So ordinary.

The doctor says her memory is delusion. The doctor says her memory is hiding her pain with fantasy. The doctor says she's almost all better, as soon as she learns to forget her face. As soon as she swallows these small oblong things, her new shape.

2. Phoenix

I am ash and mud and three red feathers left over from the war. I have a helmet. They took it from me and my scissors and shoelaces too. I want to cry out: LOOK OUT BELOW from my cocked loud beak but I touch a talon to where my song should be and there are worms. Worms and bone not my own. I want to clean, clean, clean my crimson chest but I am a flesh bag of disgusting bald, a large Aerosmith t-shirt hangs over where my pride should flutter.

What have they done? What battle have I lost this time? Why will fire no longer remedy this body of salt?

3. Dr. Shape-Shifter

Telepathically, the doctor says:

(I never said to lose your magic. I never called you dangerous. Your words not mine. Yes we have codes. Yes, we have locks. Yes, we have needles shot in your hips and cops that brought you here, and leather cuffs on beds that are not so soft. But we...we are pastel as your pills and a gentle breeze. We are safe pastures for your kind. You are not safe in the walls of the world. We can teach you how to shape shift, like me...off the job I'm an alligator. Sometimes a squirrel. So I get it—I'm one of you. Work hard play hard my friends. Turn in your liquor and needles and need for glory here and write a new story.)

The doctor says aloud: Time for art therapy!

The odd horse sleeps.

The queer bird cries:

If you take my fire, how can I be reborn?

PHOENIX SONG, VERSE THREE: THE PHOENIX TRIES TO GARDEN

1.

I do not mean The Garden
Full of apples, sin, indecision, and nostalgia.

I mean like really. I have a rental house now.
A backyard with a fig tree and inherited plants.
I should learn, right?
I tried.

I planted kale, herbs, and flowers.
They all died while I furiously outlined a screenplay.

My nature is to burn.

2.

But, the sun is fire.
The sun is plant-food.
I will die again; the sun will set.
I will rise.   Again.
As we all do.

As we all must.
And green will shoot up through topsoil,
Eager to greet
Me: odd, proud, crimson red and purple sheen,
A goofy crown and growing wingspan.
Something they can't contain.

3.

I erupt, a volcano with tail feathers
Create ashes—fertile earth—
From my own brilliant body

Years later, the soil I shed cools down
I scatter seeds in my flight onto the page.
Come, gather, eat.

THE MENTAL HEALTH SYSTEM FAILS, MUTUAL AID TRANSFORMS

The mental health system is failing us. Moreover, the way the mental health industry and our culture at large conceives of "mental illness" is designed to fail us. That's why people are more and more engaging with alternatives to it, using peer support, community, and mutual aid.

Mutual aid is not a new thing—arguably it's one of the oldest ideas in human history —but our conscious use of it in the context of mental health holds a radically important promise: rather than just coping with and adjusting to society through the mental health system, we can actually heal ourselves and shift the culture.

The biomedical model, which holds that all mental health concerns are the result of some brain imbalance, uses the oppressive tome of the Diagnostic and Statistical Manual (DSM) as its diagnostic touchstone. This gives mental health professionals the right to designate individuals who are suffering within categories of "disease," which, in turn, often assigns them to a lifetime of ineffective and often harmful "treatment." This has become so routine that it's hard to remember that alternatives to it exist, but people with mental health issues are starting re-imagine wellness. One alternative is the recovery model, an innovative and effective framework with the potential to genuinely heal and transform people who have experienced trauma.

Trauma is a huge category of human experience, ranging from the interpersonal to the systemically oppressive and often they overlap. Trauma manifests itself in various ways within our body-minds that result in types—and some of these types can be hazily recognized in the categories that the DSM describes. But this is not science. There is no evidence that supports the notion of "chemical imbalance" being something that a person is born with; this is speculation that supports a disease model, which reaps massive profits for the mental health and pharmaceutical industries.

This is not to say drugs can't be one useful treatment among many when used judiciously and cautiously. But a mental health wellness plan that begins and ends with a disease model (biomedical) does not treat the whole person, or the body, where trauma is stored, and in fact, often times causes more harm than good.

The primary tenet of the Hippocratic Oath, taken by all physicians, is "do no harm." Yet that tenet of the oath is broken over and over. These harms can include forced treatment, traumatizing hospitalizations, overmedication, and police brutality, and electroconvulsive therapy. The message of the biomedical model itself does harm to those rendered patients, and it also inhibits the personal and social transformation that could come from the recovery model and if we honored the wisdom of mutual aid.

Harm also comes from an offensive disregard for the insight and self-understanding of the person seeking professional help. There is even a word in psychiatry to denote this supposed lack of insight: anosognosia. We are thought, because of our supposedly "imbalanced" brains, to be incapable of knowing what is best for us, and thus must become compliant or "concordant" with treatment. Doctors are not a priest class, but they often act like it. Mental health professionals should be facilitators of each individual's own wellness. Progress is being made in this direction, but we have a long way to go, particularly with the majority of psychiatrists. But therapists are not immune to these problems either. In addition to the growing recovery model which offers hope that people with mental and emotional struggles can and will learn not only to cope, but to heal and thrive, we need a strengths-based model that acknowledges people who experience a range of emotions and mind-states outside the realm of "normal" may actually possess unique talents and visions, or what some call "dangerous gifts." Often this requires greater self-care. These unique perspectives we have to offer society should be cultivated and honored, not feared or stamped out.

When I couldn't find enough healing or hope or meaning in clinics, I found peer support and mutual aid in the form of 12-step community and The Icarus Project, "a support network and education project by and for people who experience the world in ways that are often diagnosed as mental illness" The Icarus Project gave me many things, most importantly friendships, and it also gave me mad pride. I now honor and mind carefully my "dangerous gifts." This is not to say therapy can't be beneficial; some of it has been. And at times, it has done me harm. But mutual aid has transformed my life, has helped me heal, and at its best, can transform society. Wikipedia solidly defines mutual aid as "a voluntary reciprocal exchange of resources and services for mutual benefit. Mutual aid, as opposed to charity, does not connote moral superiority of the giver over the receiver." In this context, therapists and psychiatrists certainly can (but don't always) embody a toxic "moral superiority," whereas people freely holding space for each others' emotional processes unlocks human potential for all involved.

When people share histories of trauma with each other, we can also share tremendous insight. Most importantly, when we create an atmosphere of mutual respect and equality that fosters wisdom and healing. In this way, mutual aid gives us something the biomedical model and the unequal power dynamics between professionals and "patients" cannot. Engaging in the very process of mutual aid itself is an antidote to the biomedical model and the flawed system it has generated.

In peer support or mutual aid, both parties look at their stuff. It seems like a no-brainer that this would promote deeper, more radical growth. It is only because we are taught not to value community that it isn't. We all know the best intimate relationships of our lives, be it with dear friends, romantic partners, or family, can make or break us—and at best can lead to profound spiritual changes. In *All About Love: New Visions* bell hooks defines love as the conscious decision to aid in the spiritual development of ourselves with another human being.

When we are in a relationship of mutual respect and equality, when the connection is between two peers struggling along the same road together, working to love one another, we can become powerful and beautiful beyond measure. I believe that mutuality can transform "patients" into people and restore health beyond expectation. More than this, I also believe that as people come into wellness and self-love, society can be transformed. As Shery Mead, founder of Intentional Peer Support writes, "As peer support in mental health proliferates, we must be mindful of our intention: social change. It is not about developing more effective services, but rather about creating dialogues that have influence on all of our understandings, conversations, and relationships."

Our healing journeys are not just about individuals. They are about transforming society and shifting the culture. In its day, The Icarus Project[1] asked: What does it mean to be labelled "crazy" in a world gone mad? And it asks if we in fact, as "mad" people, could take that label on with pride. Maybe we shouldn't adjust to this world. Maybe we should change it, not only to better serve our own needs; mad folks should support each other with mutual aid so we can better use our "dangerous gifts" to carry out visions of a just and safer future for us all.

Part of being radical involves being the best human you can be in a world not designed for love, in a world that trains us to be competitive, individualistic, selfish, hierarchical and discriminatory. Every act against that norm is a radical act. Mutual aid embodies those acts, and that is its simple yet revolutionary power.

---

[1] *In 2019, The Icarus Project ended its run, and Fireweed Collective was born. This is their mission statement: Fireweed Collective offers mental health education and mutual aid through a Healing Justice lens. We help support the emotional wellness of all people and center the needs of those most marginalized by our society. Our work seeks to disrupt the harm of systems of abuse and oppression, often reproduced by the mental health system. We strive to cultivate a culture of care, free of violence, where the ultimate goal is not just to survive, but to thrive as individuals and as communities. We envision a world in which all communities get to self-determine the source of their care, medicine, and wellness.*

NOT CONFUSED, NOT CRAZY
ON BEING A NON-BINARY
RADICAL MENTAL HEALTH
ADVOCATE

When I was nineteen, I was diagnosed with Bipolar Disorder I. I have spent much of my adult life resisting, complicating, and talking back to the damning, stigmatizing narrative of the DSM—the Diagnostic and Statistical Manual of Mental Disorders, now at edition 5. The DSM is the bible of psychiatry and the Mental Health Industrial Complex. Big Pharma is a fan. I even co-edited an anthology[2] challenging the DSM's biomedical model (with several pieces I authored). For one piece, I used a pen name because the reality of some of my "symptoms" were too scary to be open about as an untenured professor. But I have tenure now, so fuck it. I'll tell you a bit more about what has gone on in my head.

My soul, actually.

But before I do that, you should know something. This DSM document, this tome, this oppressive brick of a book that I have railed against—it *almost* got something right.

And that shudder of its near miss shook me a bit.

You see, there's another closet I'm coming out of just these past few years too. When my book had its cover in the mock-up stage, I saw my old name and winced. My name was wearing a dress. Not me. When I want to shine, I want a bowtie and a vest. Why would I put that wrong name on something I had worked so hard on? *No, that's not right.* I thought. *Not anymore, and not ever again.*

So I go by LD, or Leo to pretty much everybody now—that felt right for the cover, and it feels right for me. I identify as a masculine-of-center non-binary person. If you haven't heard this term before, non-binary is on the transgender spectrum, and it means different things to different people. I use they/them pronouns and honor the complexity of being born in a body assigned female at birth (AFAB) and having (and enjoying!) masculine as well as feminine traits, identities, presentations, etc. But lately, I'm feeling mostly masculine. Dandy and dapper, if you're curious. I have more than one pair of suspenders and loud wingtip Oxford shoes.

And yes, this process sounds fine and well, yes, dandy, but I've also slowly begun experiencing a deep, plaguing sensation of wrongness about the flesh of my chest. This feeling of disconnect between one's body and one's mind is commonly called gender dysphoria.

And whaddya know, the DSM calls it that, too.

I don't want to be classified as having a mental health disorder at all (because all of them are bogus), and now I'm saddled with two. My diagnosis of "bipolar disorder," in my opinion, is both a sensitivity towards and reaction to traumas (both personal and systemic) that yields strength, creativity, and passion, and my diagnosis of "gender dysphoria"...well that just makes me fabulous.

As my co-editor Kelechi Ubozoh and I were on tour with the book, one of my dear friends from college, who is also non-binary and trans, asked us from the audience about the DSM's entry on Gender Dysphoria. Can it be useful? I was inspired by her question. We discussed how most trans people are required to get a diagnosis of Gender Dysphoria in order to access gender affirming surgeries and hormonal therapy in our current healthcare system. This medical diagnosis makes a material difference in trans people's day-to-day lives. At the same time, the fact that gender dysphoria is in the DSM as a mental health diagnosis at all is based on a disease model that robs trans people of agency and causes us real harm. Do we need the DSM and a medical diagnosis to be there to fulfill bureaucratic needs until we have reinvented the world? After all, this isn't the only way things can be. In Uruguay the government pays for gender affirming surgery and hormonal treatment.

I realized after that event that these were important questions. It's time I consider them in writing.

So I promised you something a ways back that maybe you're curious about. I promised to let you into this curious mind/body/spirit of mine. Part of my mission in life is to tell my story as a neuroatypical psychiatric survivor to embolden and ease the suffering of others who have faced similar struggles. I want to put a human face on diagnoses like "Bipolar Disorder I" and help people understand that these categories are useless. And damaging.

All I know is that when I was 16 and I finally started coming to terms with my childhood traumas—sexual and emotional abuse—I disintegrated. I completely lost language and reason. I had symbols. I had plenty of metaphors. But I was lost to meaning because meaning was everywhere like an ocean of salt. And then I was told by doctors that what was going on was like diabetes? That I needed sedating drugs with devastating side effects for the rest of my life because I was born this way? My perpetrator found this useful as a way to remain limited in his capacity for accountability. Sadly, I believe my perpetrator has trouble thinking of himself as someone capable of doing harm. And for this reason I am not sure if he'll ever be able to be accountable and open a path for reconciliation. I can hope, but I can't count on it. So instead of recognizing the impact of his actions, he has projected the toxicity on to me, so I was "just sick." Delusional to accuse him. He said he "wanted me all the way well." Meaning, accepting I was crazy and that he was innocent would be the mark of my sanity. I genuinely hope we can come to more authentic terms with this, and each other, someday, maybe even reconcile, but that would take some major transformation from him that would allow him to admit harm done. (see "I Forgot I Remembered" and "Benediction")

Can I tell you something? I had an idea for this piece. I wanted to research and share here the entry on my particular "bipolar" diagnosis from the DSM, and feel repulsed, and tell you about it, and then you'd believe me, and I'd make this brilliant point. But I can't do that. I just tried. I couldn't do it.

I can't read the DSM entry that is used by my psychiatrist to dole out the meds that I take. (Because life is hard and I need this tool. I don't know if I'll ever be fully med-free, and that's okay.) I want to read the DSM entry to tell you this story properly, but I tremble as I consider opening a web browser with that entry. That is how much psychiatry has damaged me. Dehumanized me. Made me into a thing. Psychiatry has put me on involuntary holds in locked facilities, bound me to beds, shot me in the hip with drugs. Psychiatry continues to tell me to watch my every move, or they'll do it for me. Psychiatry doesn't expect much of me, and when I do something well, I'm an exception and a model, not a human living their life with ups and downs like everybody else. Psychiatry says I was born this way, and poor me. And see you next month, like parole. Forever.

But the truth is, "bipolar" does not come from my genes. It comes from trauma. I am certain of that. My creative resilience in response to these traumas has made me fierce, and fun, and mad, and I'm mad proud of that. Psychiatry itself has been part of what I've had to fight against, with its compounding traumas of forced medication and hospitalizations on top of the childhood traumas that brought me like a fledgling to its door. So of course I'm suspicious of the DSM and any of its attempts to "get" me. Psychiatry has gotten at me in some really violent ways. So I won't be looking up that "bipolar" diagnosis today, no thank you.

And yet.

YET.

I am less afraid to see what the DSM's entry on "Gender Dysphoria" says. Still nervous, though. I've had the triggering experience of gender dysphoria, and I've experienced microaggressions and discrimination for being non-binary. So I'm okay as I navigate the browser, but not great. But I want to answer my friend's question.

When I finally read the entry on Gender Dysphoria, a curious thing happened. When I started to read the entry, I was all IT ME. "People with gender dysphoria may be very uncomfortable with the gender they were assigned, sometimes described as being uncomfortable with their body.

People with gender dysphoria may allow themselves to express their true selves and may openly want to be affirmed in their gender identity."

Yes, thank you. THANK YOU! Thank you....DSM?!

What do I, a gender non-binary radical mental health advocate do with that?

Well I kept reading. It wasn't great. But it wasn't trash fire.

When I kept reading the entry on Gender Dysphoria in the DSM-5 I discovered two other major flaws, other than the disease model itself:

1) They use the term "opposite" gender.

Gender is a spectrum, a multi-faceted glass prism of light. There are n
opposites within a prism. At first, I felt seen, and not in a creepy way—
felt genuinely witnessed by the opening language, which was surprising
But then they reveal they think in the binary—two opposing, distinc
masculine/feminine poles—no room for complexity or nuance. FAIL.

And then I read further.

2) There's this:

"Gender dysphoria is not the same as gender nonconformity, which
refers to behaviors not matching the gender norms or stereotypes of the
gender assigned at birth. [...] Gender nonconformity is not a menta
disorder. Gender dysphoria is also not the same as being gay/lesbian.[3] "

Okay, so this is where I'm lost, and also where I think the two noted
flaws in their typology intersect. Since they see gender as a binary situation,
they are very firm that *nonconformity is not the same as dysphoria*. Huh.
What exactly could this possibly mean? They may not be the same, but
at least for me, they are undeniably intersecting experiences. I am so
befuddled by these people! The way the first part was written, it expressed
all this empathy and compassion for those "suffering" with dysphoria. But
if you're "nonconforming" that's fine, you must not be suffering, really, and
good on you.

I might be "read" as gender non-conforming when I walk around in the world because I am not on testosterone, I have not had any gender affirming surgeries, and yet I still suffer from dysphoria. My flesh feels wrong. I am uncomfortable in my skin. Where does that leave me, DSM entry?

The feeling of gender dysphoria is so rarely discussed in our culture that it feels like a welcome salve to read someone acknowledging it with compassion, and a powerful medical body no less. And dysphoria has made me suffer, so I like the compassion the DSM offers in its opening. I have grown weary of hanging bags of flesh that remind me that I'd rather be as sleek and svelte naked as I am dressed and wearing a binder. Reading the first part of the DSM entry I felt seen, acknowledged, and it didn't feel like condemnation. It felt like a ticket out of suffering. *Get this box checked, we'll get you out of that "female" box* [4.]

Yes, please! Thank you!

Maybe even write me a prescription for a medication called "Boob Be Gone!" I'd take that over the difficulty of top surgery any day, and I wouldn't feel the ambivalence I feel taking my psych drugs.

But then they continue on into knots of twisted logic in a vain attempt to make sense of something as fantastic and boundless as gender in one page.

The DSM is so good at not seeing *all* of me.

It honestly did surprise me that they offered such kind language when discussing the real pain of dysphoria, and not in a way that felt stigmatizing.

Yet its very presence in that goddamn brick of a book is a problem.

The National LGBTQ+ Task Force has this to say about the Gender Dysphoria entry in the DSM 5:

> "we must understand that as long as transgender identities are understood through a "disease" framework, transgender people suffer from unnecessary abuse and discrimination from both inside and outside the medical profession. As long as gender variance is characterized by the medical field as a mental condition, transgender people will find their identities invalidated by claims that they are "mentally ill," and therefore not able to speak objectively about their own identities and lived experiences."[4]

First of all, thank you. Transgender and non-binary identities are not "mental illnesses." But where does this leave me, Task Force? Are you going to throw me under the bus with my "legit mental illness"—and say that I am, by virtue of it, not able to speak objectively about my own identity and lived experience? There is a word for this: "anosognosia." That's what psychiatrists say when they don't want to listen to their patients. The idea is that we can't be trusted to know our own truth because we're too damaged to know what's good for us. Sounds remarkably like my perpetrator and his own heartbreaking, ironic delusions—he thinks I am "too sick" to be trusted with the truth, and I say he simply cannot be trusted—at least not until he is accountable. We with lived mental health experience are the ones who should be listened to the most. Nothing about us without us.

As a radical mental health advocate, I have argued that every so-called "disease" in the DSM is a reaction to trauma.

Louder for the people in the back: *As a proud non-binary person, I do not believe trans or non-binary identity is connected to trauma other than the fact that trans and non-binary people endure the traumas of bigotry and institutional cis-supremacy. Trans and non-binary identity is not borne of trauma, but we are certainly subject to it, and to say otherwise is itself bigoted.* A non-binary friend of mine had to fire a therapist who tried to link their gender to their childhood trauma. That therapeutic rupture itself was traumatic for my friend.

My critique of the inclusion of Gender Dysphoria in the DSM does not come from the same place as my critique of other entries, such as "bipolar disorder." My work as a mental health advocate has given me language to counter the biomedical model; there is "the recovery model" which claims that our wounds can be healed, and with the right trauma-informed care those who struggle with their moods or wellness won't always be reliant on drugs and oppressive institutions.

But obviously, "recovery from trauma" is not the answer for what is described as "Gender Dysphoria." Trans and non-binary are valid identities, not diseases.

But no one with mental health struggles has a disease.

As a person marked as "mentally ill," I also have a positive identity that I share with others marked in this way. We are mad, we are neuorodivergent. We are not wrong. We represent a different kind of diversity—we share the sufferings of our traumas, the sensitivity and creativity of our beings, the shared struggle of seeking care from institutions that harm. We live in the margins of the mind.

The LGBTQ+ Task Force would probably say this is just another historical moment to fight the bigotry of the American Psychiatric Association on behalf of trans and non-binary people. Lesbian and gay identity were in the DSM-3. Social movements and pride wiped them out. But there is a crucial distinction here. For lesbian, gay and bisexual folks, the DSM said the "condition" of homosexuality needed to be "cured"—which led to the horror that is conversion therapy. But for Gender Dysphoria, the DSM recommends a "cure" of gender affirming surgery and/or hormone treatment, *which is often what the patients actually want.* This makes a world of difference.

But what if we did more than take out the Gender Dysphoria entry from the DSM? What if we acknowledged the intersection of the oppressions of trans and non-binary people and neuroatypical people? That intersection certainly lives in me. As Audre Lorde said of her intersections: "which me will survive all these liberations?"

What if we threw the brick of a book out of a window? What if we replaced it with as many explanations for our minds and identities and bodies as there are people? What if we honored and celebrated everyone's individual story?

Some trans and non-binary folks might say of their experience:

"My gender is on a spiritual journey" or "My trans body is part of nature's biodiversity" or "My gender just is how it is and it's only colonialism and/ or monotheism which denies it." And on and on, through the prism.

And here is the crucial intersection. This is similar to the rhetoric I and others use about our experience as people with diagnoses of "mental illness": "My mind isn't breaking down, I'm experiencing a spiritual emergence because I have dangerous gifts." "My mind is part of nature's neurodiversity." "My mind is on a shamanic quest." And on and on, through a different prism.

But like double helixes, my non-binary gender and my identity and my body and my brilliance and my madness are all inextricably bound together, and unique. A psychiatrist would just pen down that I have two diagnoses. I would say I have multiple resiliences and brilliances. And my own story to tell.

As much as I want to throw the DSM through a window and call for a revolution in mental health care and gender, I also know those windows are shut pretty tight. Don't get me wrong, I do want to overthrow cis-hetero-patriarchal white supremacist imperialist ableist sanist capitalism. I just think we need healing and whole people to do it, and a whole lot of us.

Here's the revolution I want to call for in gender and mental health: let's repurpose all those books (and lord, there are so many) into actual bricks and build community centers and hospitals that offer free surgery and hormones on demand without need of any permission slip, as well as mutual aid groups for anyone trying to survive this world and all its boxes—especially the ones with locks on them.

[2] *We've Been Too Patient: Voices from Radical Mental Health—Stories and Research Challenging the Biomedical Model* edited by LD Green and Kelechi Ubozoh, North Atlantic Books, 2019

[3] https://www.psychiatry.org/patients-families/gender-dysphoria/what-is-gender-dysphor

[4] https://www.thetaskforce.org/invalidating-transgender-identities-progress-and-trouble-ir the-dsm-5/

COMING BACK AROUND TO BI

(After Miriam Zoila Perez's "Coming Back Around to Butch" from
Persistence: All Ways Butch and Femme)

There's a box where my anxiety lives. This box is on OK Cupid. To check, or not to check: "I do not want to see or be seen by straight people." A friend of mine quipped that it is the most satisfying box to check on the internet. Maybe for them. For me it is fraught with tension and complexity. I have checked and unchecked this box many times—this box that determines whether or not I am categorically, exclusively queer. Here, on OKCupid of all places, is a way to express a subcultural value of separatist politics. But I get it. Sometimes checking the box feels safer, or just smarter. When I don't have the box checked, the majority of my inbox is filled with cis straight men I would never even meet for coffee with vaguely harassing opening salvos like "Hey pretty." At best.

There were times in my life when I was certain that there were subtle, yet critical lines in the sand between queers and everyone else. I wanted to reject the more mainstream "bisexual" label and own the subversive potential of "queer." I thought perhaps if I did there would be some kind of initiation ceremony where I'd get to ride a unicorn through a rainbow and emerge with iridescent skin that only other queers could recognize, and I'd never be without love, friendship, and community again. And I'd have cooler clothes.

But in reality, I have had sexual and romantic relationships with men and women, cis and trans* folks, straights and queers. And this is the thing about occupying the space bisexual that I think is politically significant. We are not just switch hitters, we are ambassadors between cultures. It's part of why we're stigmatized for being double agents. But it's a special, important, albeit difficult position. This is why I'm coming back around to bi.

In queer culture, we want to abandon the binary altogether, or at least play with it, but most of the world is still split in two. How do we accommodate this? "Bisexual" is a term straight people know. It has cultural currency in their world. Sure, I'm not thrilled with the representation of Tila Tequila on *A Shot at Love*, but hey, at least it's out there. At least this show can help straight people get on page one of the queer primer: it's not just about who you sleep with, it's who you fall in love with. But Tila never said she was "queer." She owned "bisexual"— perhaps playing into an overly sexualized, feminized stereotype, but nonetheless, she owned this position of not only desiring, but also emotionally connecting with people across the gender spectrum. That got people watching, thinking, and talking.

Now, Tila Tequila's first queer reality dating show was twelve years ago. Since then, a string of celebrities have come out as bi, including Anna Paquin, Lady Gaga, Alan Cumming, Megan Fox, Billie Joe Armstrong, Carrie Brownstein, and Drew Barrymore, and dozens more, to be sure. Certainly, the mainstream cultural climate for LGBTQ+ folks has shifted in the past nine years of the fight for gay marriage and in the aftermath of that ultimate victory. It seems the zeitgeist is now allowing for more complex conversations about gender, sexuality and identity to happen. With this, trans* issues are gaining much needed awareness, and more people are claiming "bisexual" rather than gay or straight. Julia Serano, an important transwoman writer (author of the widely read, quoted, referenced, and syllabized manifestos on trans* identity) notes in her book *Excluded: Making Feminist and Queer Movements More Inclusive* that trans* folks and bisexuals have often been allies. They are two groups (sometimes overlapping in one body, such as mine, as gender and sexuality are not the same thing) who have historically been demonized by certain gays, lesbians and radical feminists.

For me, using the word "queer" within the LGBTQ+ community was partially a way to protect myself from biphobia. But I think that needs to be addressed head-on. But for the straight community, the word "queer" is a bit more obscure than "bisexual." Which is not to say we shouldn't use it, especially if it feels more true, or if people don't want to be ambassadors. I just don't think "bisexual" should be abandoned.

Dan Savage tries to be the gay guy straights can relate to. He's doing his part, along with bisexuals, to bridge the gap—although he's pretty biphobic himself. For this and other reasons, he pisses me off fairly routinely, but I've got to hand it to him on one point. One time I heard him speak, and he offered: "What would it be like if cis men asked their female partners: what are you into? And what if the answer was—well

I'm not always that into penetration."

I think most cis straight men's heads would explode. Or at least, this would be a deal-breaker with regards to sexual intimacy.

Queer people, in general, are part of a culture where folks negotiate their desires. For most straight people, phallocentric vaginal sex is just assumed to be the main course. The event that all other sexual activity leads up to. And it can be a spectacular meal. With detachable dildos or their fleshy counterparts. But it shouldn't have to be the only option for satiation.

The obvious thing to note here is that I took some Women's Studies (and there I'm showing my age, as they were not "Gender Studies" yet) classes in college, what with the use of "phallocentric" and all. But it's not just feminism. Desire isn't that political. Right? Desire is often about power, but that's not the same as politics.

Or...is desire a decision you can make, a lifestyle you commit to based on principles, like being a vegetarian? Is love a choice? If desire were strictly political, then this would be the moment I pass through the rainbow. I would embrace the label "queer" wholeheartedly and vow to never date or sleep with a cis straight dude again[5]. But this strikes me as similar to that old saying in the seventies: "feminism is the theory, lesbianism is the practice." I think that got retired for a reason. But what about that other '70s classic: "the personal is political."

I couldn't agree more.

If I feel tangible desire for men, both cis and trans* alike, doesn't it help the cause of all people for me to bring my queer sensibilities and feminism into the sacred space of the bedroom?

Don't we need ambassadors?

Sex isn't always what we want it to be. That can range from the dissatisfying to the violent. Ambassadors can help with this. One of my favorite spoken word poets, Andrea Gibson, has a line about stopping rape. Gibson says: "She's not asking what you're going to tell your daughter/She's asking what you're going to teach your son."

We don't all have sons to teach. But for those of us who want to take male lovers, there are lessons here to give and receive. Of course, not all heterosexual sex is like rape. But it sometimes is. Sometimes in subtle, pernicious, and corrosive ways. Sometimes in overt, traumatic ones. Roxane Gay's 2018 anthology, *Not That Bad: Dispatches from Rape Culture*, speaks to this reality just in the title. And I don't have to give you statistics here. We all know that rape happens most often with people who already know each other. And while it's true that sometimes women and queers are the perpetrators of intimate partner violence, I also don't need statistics to affirm that the vast majority of the time, rape is done by cisgender straight men. Rape culture is systemic. We need to build a culture of consent, and queer culture, with its norms of negotiating desires, offers this.

The shape and quality of the love feels different between queers and across the lavender bridge into the straight world. But one is not more or less worthy than the other.

When I claimed earlier: "I'm not bi, I'm queer, and I only date queers" I drew a perimeter that excluded cis straight guys. When really, they are the ones who need a handful of glitter and consent the most. More than that, claiming queer-only as my identity denies the real love I've shared with cis straight men[6]. It makes me feel like a fraud, inadequate. My "hetero" relationships are not just something in my past to gloss over, ask forgiveness for. It erases my history to do so, which still lives within me. My past informs my present and future. I don't want to disrespect it. I need it to feel whole.

If anyone does need to draw a line to exclude the cis and the straight and the dude, like I once did, that's fine. Or if they need to exclude any sex or gender to love. That's cool. I can respect that. I just ask that they respect the label bisexual, because for me, it is a label that affirms my appetite as an omnivore. My appetite to explore my own dandy-masculine gender with a full range of genders. This feels integral to who I am. This multiplicity of desire is perhaps not a choice in the same way that being gay or being straight is not a choice. It's anybody's guess.

So this is where my two labels meet. For the sake of doing my part to queer the world with a culture of consent, I am coming back around to bi. With a caveat: a queer to some, a bisexual to others. Depending on who I am talking to, and what language they speak. I am an ambassador, after all.

I'm coming back around to: Hi there. There's plenty of room on the back of this unicorn. Let's ride through this rainbow together.

---

5   Note: I wrote this essay a while ago, when I identified as a cis woman, and before I came out as a trans-masculine non-binary person. If a cis dude slept with me now, I mean...that's not straight. But was it ever? See footnote 6.

6   As spacetime speaks back to the cis-body I once was (?), and the trans*-body I am now (!), do all those historical "hetero" relationships also become queered? Can I even really say I was always cis, or was I always in the process of becoming the (more) stable star matter I am today? Do my cis straight men exes need to come out? Are my cis women queer exes now bi or pan if they weren't before? How do we locate ourselves on a chronology of shifting genders and desires? For five years I have been partnered with a non-binary trans femme. I love the idea that our genders together, and our intimacy together, transcends space and time. T4T=astrophysics. (See also my prose poem: "Event Horizons").

THE PHOENIX MOLTS[7]

The Group. They were misfits. Mystics. Changemakers. Dreambreakers. You know, poets. And not just any poets. Slam Poets. Hard to define, together or singly. I couldn't say I didn't know The Group entirely. I mean I'd slept with two of them.

I was one of them, too—a hatchling under their wings. Tender little baby dyke. I am settled in my skin and glittery feathers, now. I shine on stages still here and there, but my real work is to shelter my own hatchlings (students) for a living, and I love it.

Let me tell you about the night I molted from awkward, fledgling, open-mouth bird, to bright champion of torch flight.

At the last national festival in Phoenix, before the continental empire disbanded into regional tournaments and fifteen minutes of flame, a band of us broke off from the revelry of the hotel lobby. You know, after the after party. Our teams had lost, and we were stressed and depressed. Me? Bored, lonely, a little drunk. Stress was a lifestyle for me, not situational. We found our way to a public restroom...the men's and women's rooms on each side of a corridor of white painted wood. I hung back and watched, so lonely that I'd actually brought out some knitting. I was making a rainbow vest for my cat for pride.

The rest of the group. They were up to something. I didn't know what.

These misfits, these mystics, they changed my life that night.

Knitting stitch by knitting stitch, I witnessed them from the safety of a few yards:

 *not a single file line, their grade school teachers would not be proud
 *a spectrum of drunkenness, but everyone? At least a little.
 *AND THIS: they mill through the corridor, going from the Men's to Women's and back again
 *laughter, shouts...wailing?
 *a lavender glow emanates from either side of the bathrooms' entrances

I tucked my knitting away in a teal leather bag that purported to be a purse, but was really designed to hold all the accoutrements of my craft. I slung it over my shoulder, tiptoeing over to the action in my ballerina flats. I caught a glimpse of myself in the lobby's mirror walls. Ripped jeans, baggy shirt, a haircut somewhere between a pixie and a rough lesbian shag. Heavy black eyeliner. You could say my kindling wings were already getting ready, even if I wasn't.

The crew was doubled over, laughing, or splayed out, spent, relaxed, literally feeding each other grapes like lavish Romans.

Just yards away, but I knew I would have to fly to get to them and the bright world they occupied. I caught the glance of dapper Blair, one of my former lovers, whose mouth curled in recognition at my gaze. I almost dropped my glance, but instead I called out across the divide:

"Which side do I start from?"

"Either! Both!" said the boi Joe I also Knew, they of curly hair and boisterous booming voice.

I poked my head inside the bathroom corridor adjoining the Men's and Women's entrances.

A soft, glowing, pink, white and blue cloud hovered in the middle.

"I put a spell on you," Alize, a high femme trans woman sang the Nina Simone lyric.

"No way it was totally a team piece," Joe rejoined, throwing an arm around Alize. *Wow, it had only been a week since we'd happened—was Alize next?* More laughter.

I moved my way through the cloud. It was not wet, or sticky, just bright, and warm and radiant and it moved through my solar plexus until my chest could not expand any more or shrink any less.

I moaned. Yes, that kind of moan.

"No shame in the game!" Blair called out. He'd heard me moan like that before. Not sure if that made it better or worse.

I decided to trust them. I kept walking through the cloud until I got to the other side. To join them.

But when I got through, they had all vanished.

"Hello?" I paused. "Guys?"

I looked down. I had a flat chest—a beaming board! (Yes, yes, at last). I rubbed my hands up and down...no. Nothing there, not even scars. I looked in the mirror. I had a chiseled jaw, five o'clock shadow, hair buzzed on both sides and an impressive pompadour.

Same clothes though.

That made it worse, not better. My body was a GQ catalog but my style was still Urban Outfitters, from both sides of the store.

Both sides.

I had to go through again.

And back the other way.

And stumbling through again.

And then flying back through a door frame that seemed to shrink.

And then falling in fear in the other direction.

And then climbing and falling and then flying and then soaring and each time releasing a moan deeper, more resonant, until I finally came, and came tumbling out to find my friends and lovers again.

"Hey," I said to them all, fists on hips. My voice was low and gravelly. "Welcome to my cotillion."

They froze, stared at me. Janelle Monae kept playing. They didn't say a word.

Finally, Joe laughed. "You're the beau of the ball."

Blair approached and spun me around and dipped me to the floor. I extended my arm with a grace I'd never felt before.

I still had the killer new body, and the bold haircut...and the same both-sides clothes.

But it's okay this time.

Better than okay.

This time I see foot hair piping up through ballerina flats, and I love it.

This time my body released a spark and it burned my fear and shame to ash.

This time I ignite, fly, radiant, free.

---

[7] A pack of lies chasing the truth.

A LETTER TO MY DILDO

You are only for special occasions.

Everyday use is external, anxious rub-out high powered
Hitachi Magic Wand.
But you, dear dildo, pink and soft, pseudo-skin
Bendable core—you
Live in a harness
Ready for the nights I am feeding you to another's welcoming maw.
But you, dear dildo,
have not found much occasion to do this of late.

Dear dildo,
curious model of an appendage
That is usually shrunken
You are comically large, extended, and chronically hard.
Once I found you inside of me at the hands
Of a lover who would have me worship his cock.
Dear dildo, you are not an ersatz penis.
You are not a faux phallus.
You are not Pinocchio.

You thrill the Blue Fairy just as you are.

When this man could embrace your utility—
Pleasure and engulfment of my core
Without concern for his raw nerve—
This was magic and beauty.
And when we put you away, dear dildo
My heart went with you.

His body shrunk down to eight inches of flesh
Sweating and holding and forcing

I mention this as a brick, a Bible, and a block of wood—
I have few other words but these here.

Dear dildo, I missed you while I was away

He asked me if I'd used you on another woman.
(Typical)
Yes, I'd said.
But no, not use.
Dear dildo, you are a gift.
You parody the paradox.
You sweet grace,

You plastic, elastic, ecstatic thing,
Dear dildo, at best you make us sing,
Dear dildo, this is my offering
From a body who goes in with you
and will take you in, too.
With your selfless generosity,
You are what the cock should be.

BENEDICTION

My last book, *We've Been Too Patient: Voices from Radical Mental Health—Stories and Research Challenging the Biomedical Model,* co edited with Kelechi Ubozoh, showcased a chorus of resilience and survivorship from the mental health system itself from many people of diverse backgrounds.

In that book in front of you I, and others, assert the idea that so-called mental health "disorders" are reactions to trauma, including childhood trauma.

In this book, I share my response and resilience to traumas—childhood traumas, and psychiatric traumas, and gender-based violence, and transphobic and queerphobic violence. Some are Traumas, some are traumas, and some are anywhere in between.

I also embody my sexuality and gender expression and identity. Humbly, curiously, inconclusively, I put these strands of my soul next to each other and let you, dear reader, decide what to do with their juxtaposition. I don't have all the answers, I just know what I've known, you know?

In my personal computer archive, and in versions of this manuscript, there are pieces I chose not to include in this final publication for complex and personal reasons.

These pieces—at turns poetically, at turns in prose—elucidate more on my childhood traumas.

Perhaps a future book will help me weave together a new story to help me heal from what I experienced then...

...the stories we tell ourselves to make sense of our wounds don't always last throughout our lives, and the pieces I left out no longer serve me.

Naming who hurt me in a public forum is not the road to healing right now, and that's what the removed pieces did.

In the spirit of Restorative Justice, the person harmed gets to decide when and how accountability takes place. Now is not the time, and I don't think a public forum will ever be the right path for me with these particular injuries. I am more than happy to publicly and loudly stand up to the mental health industrial complex, cis-heteropatriarchy, ableism, white supremacy, and other systems of oppression, but for many reasons, I do not want to make a case against or expose who hurt me through the publication of this writing, and perhaps that is never going to be the way for me.

I will lend my voice to the chorus of other survivors, though, in what way I can.

So, for the sake of this volume's meaning-making I do need to clearly state that my mental health struggles originate with childhood trauma—sexual and emotional abuse.

I did not make it up. I am not delusional. I am not diseased. I am wounded. Diagnoses attempt to describe scar tissue, not innate flaws or born-with "imbalances." They fail even to do that. Poetry and narrative not only help us understand the wounds, they can even write us out of them, into community, out of isolation, into healing. But to name who hurt me publicly might injure me again. And I have not given up hope of some measure of reconciling, so in this case I think there is a measured use of silence.

I will say: I survived, and I am not alone.

You are not alone.

READING GUIDE

Theme: **Uses of Humor**

We all love to laugh. Laughter heals, laughter brings people together, and can even challenge oppression...when it's punching up, not punching down. Meaning, the capacity to make people laugh is a kind of power, and with power comes responsibility (or so Spiderman was told). To be ethical with humor, we laugh at ourselves, or laugh at people with more power than us, but never at the expense of people who are oppressed. And the best humor often comes from our own pain, as a way to release it and offer release to the reader or audience who shares that pain. Or it can offer a bridge to empathy for those who haven't shared that particular pain, but understand the universal suffering that yields the laughter.

Prompt
Think of a day or night where nothing went according to plan, or just didn't go your way.

What did you want?

Why couldn't you get it?

Write from that frustration—a story or a poem and tell the tale of that day or night with a beginning, middle and end.

Representative Poems

that illustrate use of humor are:

Representative Prose

that illustrate use of humor are:

Theme: **Gender**

Some of us take our gender for granted to be more or less in alignment with social expectations of the sex we were assigned at birth, and some of us go through a journey of discovery around our gender, and this can change and evolve throughout our lifetimes.

Prompt
What about you is not in alignment with the "script" of what a man or woman should be, or what a boy or girl should be?

Have you ever experienced "the gender police" coming after you for not following the script?

What was that like?

Write about that experience and how it has shaped you and your sense of yourself?

and/or

If you could go back in time, what would you tell your childhood self about your gender journey ahead?

Representative Poems
that illustrate use of gender are:

o "Event Horizons" (p. 6)

o "Lady Macbeth to Octomom" (p. 8)

o "Letter to My Dildo" (p. 73)

Representative Prose
that illustrate use of gender are:

o "Not Confused, Not Crazy: On Being a Non-Binary Radical Mental Health Advocate" (p. 44)

Theme: **Sexuality**

Sex can be a powerful form of healing and release and a potent life force that connects people with their purpose and passion and drive, and even destiny. When society shames people for their relationship to their sexuality, it can be soul-crushing. But the reclamation of one's sexual self can be a powerful medicine. (Of course, sex is not for everybody, or it can wax and wane in importance in a person's life, and that's fine!)

Prompt
So much of sexuality is grounded in sensuality—the five senses.

Write out five columns for all five senses—sight, sound, taste, smell, touch, and make a long list for each of the sensations that give you pleasure, and dip a little erotic at least once or twice.

Write a poem based on them.

For me:

the color teal, the sound of onions sizzling in olive oil, the taste of coffee with sugar and milk, the smell of menstrual blood, the feel of a buzzed head on my palm.

Representative Poems

that illustrate use of sexuality are:

- o "Apples and Oranges" (p. 1)
- o "Pomegranate" (p. 23)
- o "Letter to My Dildo" (p. 37)

Representative Prose

that illustrate use of sexuality are:

- o "Body to Machine" (p. 13)
- o "Coming Back Around to Bi" (p. 59)
- o "The Phoenix Molts" (p. 67)

Theme: **Trauma, Memory, and Space-TIme**

When you reflect on difficult things that have happened to you in your life, how has the memory persisted or failed to persist?   How do you relate to your former self that experienced the hardship? What is the relationship between memory and trauma and space-time?

Prompt
Think of a difficult moment in your life. Create two pages, one for then, one for now.

Then page: What year was it? What month? What season? How old were you? What smells do you remember? What objects? What other sights, sounds, sensations?

Now page: What year is it now? What month? What season? How old are you? What smells are in this room? What objects? What other sights, sounds, sensations?

Take a look at both pages and choose from the responses to craft a poem or piece of prose.

Representative Poems
that illustrate use of Trauma, Memory, and Space-Time are:

Representative Prose

that illustrate use of Trauma, Memory, and Space-Time are:

- o "The Mental Health System Fails, Mutual Aid Transforms"
  (p. 38)
- o Not Confused, Not Crazy: On Being a Non-Binary Radical
  Mental Health Advocate" (p. 44)

Theme: **Mental Health**

The pandemic has made this ever more evident: there are not two categories of people—"the mentally ill" and the "sane." We all struggle to some degree with our mental health, and need to take care of each other and not rely exclusively on limited or failing systems. Mental health systems can be as traumatic as the original wounds they are supposed to be healing. These systems frequently have a "biomedical model" rather than a trauma-informed model, prescribing medication and damning with life-long "diagnosis" rather than trying to truly heal with somatic-based care, or with other modalities that get to the root of the issues. And then there's overmedicating, and how societal oppressions like racism and transphobia play out with the DSM and pharmaceutical industry. Not to mention the problems with insurance, access to care, and the fact that the majority of therapists and psychiatrists are culturally insensitive to BIPOC and queer and trans* communities. And fundamentally, there is this fear of "madness" in our culture that dates back to the enlightenment; poetry in our lives and from the margins of our minds are seen as threatening to the supremacy of "reason." The so-called "mad" are often frustrated seers, visionaries who must learn to tend to their "dangerous gifts" carefully and lovingly. The "mentally ill" are much more likely to be the victims of violence than the perpetrators of it. Some of the violence is forced hospitalization.

Prompt
What is your experience with your mental health?

What helps you?

What causes more harm?

Make a list of your favorite self care activities.

They can be "boring" or simple—brushing your teeth. Or more elaborate—meditation, baking.

How do your close friendships or relationships support your mental health?

Make a second list of dear ones in your life and a third list of something—a quality, a concrete object, a creative collaboration, that this dear one brings to your life.

From these three lists, write a poem of resilience.

Representative Poems

that illustrate use of Mental Health are:

- o "Apples and Oranges" (p. 1)
- o "Sometimes I Slip" (p. 20)
- o "Finding the Signal" (p. 25)
- o "I Forgot I Remembered" (p. 27)
- o "Phoenix Song" (p. 32)

Representative Prose

that illustrate use of Mental Health are:

- o "The Mental Health System Fails, Mutual Aid Transforms" (p. 38)
- o "Not Confused, Not Crazy: On Being a Non-Binary Radical Mental Health Advocate" (p. 44)

ACKNOWLEDGMENTS

As mentioned in the introduction, this is a book over fifteen years in the making. It's impossible to catalogue all the people who encouraged me, lifted me up, or just saw me, really met me over these years. Or the institutions, editors, and publishers who have made a difference in my writing journey. Whether you are in my life now frequently, intermittently, or mostly in memory, please know that you matter to me.

So I'll try.

College dears, Meredith Summs and Ainsley Story. I'll never stop thanking you!

A college companion, a good egg: thanks for being you, Patrick Whittle.

The man who got me into slam—JT Bullock. Big thanks!

So many people in the Bay Area slam poetry community where I cut my teeth and supported me in that intense growth spurt. Too many to name all of them, such a wonderful ecosystem I am grateful to have blossomed within. Julia Serano—thank you for the read and the blurb!

And from that era of my life, thank you for witnessing and supporting me: the Beckett's crew, again, too many to name, another lovely microclimate.

Thank you Julia Hazer, a bright enduring light in my life. I am so glad we're friends.

Then grad school and queer ensemble theater era. Especially Oscar Ruiz. I am ever-grateful.

Lambda Literary and Icarus Project and Queer Open Mic era— Jacks McNamara and Jen Stanley. Miss you both in New Mexico! And Baruch Porras-Hernandez, so grateful to know you and to benefit from how you build community. Thank you to Nicola Griffith and Ellery Washington for mentorship and inspiration, and so much deep gratitude for Ellery's blurb.

Susannah Layton—thank you for your friendship and supporting my artistry in those years, too.

July Westhale, thank you for being a steady friend for years, and for your feedback on an early version of this manuscript, and for publishing *Not Confused, Not Crazy* in PULP.

Sonya Renee Taylor, you gave an old slam friend a chance to write for *The Body is Not an Apology (TBINAA)*. You saw me smoldering in the ashes. Grateful to know you, and thank you for publishing my work.

Erin Wiegand, dear friend extraordinaire, you believed in what you saw that I published on TBINAA, and you helped launch *We've Been Too Patient*. So much gratitude.

Kelechi Ubozoh, where to begin. Co-editing our book was a joy and a journey, and its life in the world is thrilling, and our friendship continues on this wonderful path. Thank you for being this book's doula, and for the read and the blurb.

Thank you friends/colleagues for your support of me as a professional and person: the Los Medanos College English Department, and especially Morgan Lynn, George Olgin, and Jill Buettner. And to extended LMC and 4CD friends—Nick Garcia, James Noel, Briana McCarthy, Melissa Pon, Adam Bessie, Sabrina Kwist, and Nina Ghiselli.

Thank you more friends Shane Fairchild, Eli Conley (and thank you for coaching me through and editing *Not Confused, Not Crazy*), Meg Schoerke, J Cohen, Stella Sheldon, Dev Cuny, Katherine Mancuso, Elana Isaacs, Liana Harden, Amy Goldman, Sean Chandra, and Isaac Fellman.

Screenwriting buddies, such fun with you I have. Melanie Mockobey, Conor Dowling, Joey Povinelli, Alex Knell, and the rest of the crew... thank you for being on the writers' journey with me. Thanks to Ramon Parada and Senda Rios, for raising such a wonderful person! And for being supportive and welcoming.

Thank you so much to Meg Elison for all the support, the blurb, and help with *The Phoenix Molts*.

Thank you to L. Harris for the read and the blurb and being a rad mental health writer comrade.

Thanks Melissa Eleftherion Carr for the lovely blurb, and for introducing me to Diane Di Prima in that wonderful workshop. Thank you to Diane, rest in power.

Thanks: to Mills College MFA in Creative Writing—to Elmaz Abinader, Marc Bamuthi Joseph, Kirsten Saxton, and to Justin Chin— rest in power. To Tin House and Elissa Schappell. To Catwalk Artists' Residency Program.

So much gratitude to North Atlantic Books for how you supported me, Kelechi, and We've Been Too Patient. Thanks especially to Bevin Donahue, Alison Knowles, and Lorna Garano. Thanks especially to Lorna for being such a fine editor to "The Mental Health System Fails, Mutual Aid Transforms" which is included in this volume.

Thank you to *Salon, PULP Magazine, Sinister Wisdom, Foglifter, and sPARKLE & bLINK* and quiet lightning, *The Mad Studies Reader,* and *The Body is Not an Apology* for the reprints.

Thank you to Miah Jeffra, good buddy and truly gifted editor of this book, a midwife, truly.

Thank you to J. K. Fowler, Laura Salazar, and the Nomadic Press team for believing in my work and publishing it! I'm honored and so grateful.

Thank you to my parents Peter Donahue and Susan Donahue for believing in me and supporting me and instilling in me tenacity and the habits of creativity. I love you both.

Thank you to my sister Tana Green for her model of bravery, kindness and strength. I love you.

Salaams, so much appreciation for our friendship, and for our creativity, laughter, and mercurial banter.

Ramon(a), you are my anchor and safe harbor. You are my singing heart and 72 degree sun. I love you, endlessly.

LD Green

LD (Leo) Green is a queer and non-binary writer, performer, college educator, and mental health advocate living in Richmond, California. They co-edited the anthology *We've Been Too Patient: Voices from Radical Mental Health* with Kelechi Ubozoh, published in 2019 by North Atlantic Books. Leo's work has been published on *Salon, Mad in America, The Body is Not an Apology*, truth-out.org, in Sinister Wisdom, Foglifter, and elsewhere. They have received fellowships from Lambda Literary, Tin House, and Catwalk Artists in Residence. Leo has placed as a quarterfinalist and semifinalist in two international screenwriting contests. They are pitching a YA science fiction novel, and adapting one of their screenplays into a graphic novel. Leo teaches composition, literature, and creative writing at Los Medanos College.

OTHER WAYS TO SUPPORT NOMADIC PRESS' WRITERS

In 2020, two funds geared specifically toward supporting our writers were created: the **Nomadic Press Black Writers Fund** and the **Nomadic Press Emergency Fund**.

The former is a forever fund that puts money directly into the pockets of our Black writers. The latter provides dignity-centered emergency grants to any of our writers in need.

Please consider supporting these funds. You can also more generally support Nomadic Press by donating to our general fund via nomadicpress.org/donate and by continuing to buy our books.

As always, thank you for your support!

Scan below for more information and/or to donate.
You can also donate at nomadicpress.org/store.